100 AMAZING FACTS ABOUT PIRATES

© 2023, Marc Dresgui

Content

Introduction 8
Fact 1 - Blackbeard's Riddle 9
Fact 2 - Anne Bonny, the Terror of the Seas 10
Fact 3 – Why Pirates Wore Earrings................................. 11
Fact 4 - The Mystery of the Hidden Treasures 12
Fact 5 - The Secret Language of Pirates 13
Fact 6 – The Strict Rules of Pirate Code 14
Fact 7 - How Pirates Read the Stars 15
Fact 8 - The True Face of Calico Jack 16
Fact 9 - Where does "Jolly Roger" come from?.............. 17
Fact 10 - Pirates and their parrots 18
Fact 11 - The Map That Leads to the Priceless 19
Fact 12 - The Courage of Mary Read, Pirate................... 20
Fact 13 - The Dance of Swords on the Bridge 21
Fact 14 - Did the pirates really eat cookies?................... 22
Fact 15 - How to avoid seasickness 23
Fact 16 - The Secrets of the Ghost Ships........................ 24
Fact 17 - Pirates and Their Mystical Tattoos 25
Fact 18 - Turtle Island, the Privateers' Lair 26
Fact 19 - Who were the Buccaneers?.............................. 27
Fact 20 - A Pirate Foamer's Life.. 28
Fact 21 - The Mysterious Pirate Lady of China 29
Fact 22 - Captain Kidd's Lost Treasure............................ 30

Fact 23 - Techniques for Spotting a Ship 31

Fact 24 - How Pirates Avoided Sharks 32

Fact 25 - Pirates' Favorite Musical Instruments 33

Fact 26 - The surprising role of cats on board 34

Fact 27 - The Amazing Friendship Between Pirates and Turtles . 35

Fact 28 - Secret Codes on Cards 36

Fact 29 - Techniques to avoid capture 37

Fact 30 - Were the Pirates Really Lawless? 38

Fact 31 - The Mystery of the Wooden Legs 39

Fact 32 - The Legends of Sir Francis Drake 40

Fact 33 - The Compass, Pirates' Precious Friend 41

Fact 34 - Alliances between pirates and natives 42

Fact 35 - Blackbeard's True Loot 43

Fact 36 - Amulets to protect against storms 44

Fact 37 - Pirates and Seabirds 45

Fact 38 - The Great Pirate Prison Escape 46

Fact 39 - Secret Signals Between Pirate Ships 47

Fact 40 - Strange Animals on Board Ships 48

Fact 41 - The Secret Recipe for Pirate Rum 49

Fact 42 - Pirates in the Panama Canal 50

Fact 43 - The Art of Negotiation in Pirates 51

Fact 44 - Pirate Remedies for Scurvy 52

Fact 45 - The Role of Women in the Golden Age 53

Fact 46 - Pirates and Their Amazing Jewels 54

Fact 47 - The First Female Pirate Captain 55

Fact 48 - The World's Most Wanted Treasures 56

Fact 49 - Life Aboard a Ship in Combat 57

Fact 50 - Privateers, Heroes or Pirates 58

Fact 51 - How Pirates Hid Their Loot 59

Fact 52 - The Mysteries of the South Seas 60

Fact 53 - Technique for Boarding a Ship 61

Fact 54 - Pirates and their board games 62

Fact 55 - Buccaneers' Favorite Songs 63

Fact 56 - Pirates and Voodoo Magic 64

Fact 57 - The Invention of Treasure Maps 65

Fact 58 - Pirates' Navigational Instruments 66

Fact 59 - Pirates and their funny superstitions 67

Fact 60 - The Amazing Friendships Between Pirates and Kings. 68

Fact 61 - The Mysterious Treasure of Cocos Island 69

Fact 62 - Pirates and their singular mascots 70

Fact 63 - Legendary rivalries between captains 71

Fact 64 - Pirates and their frenzied dances 72

Fact 65 - The Secrets of Bottles in the Sea 73

Fact 66 - Pirates and their underground hideouts 74

Fact 67 - Techniques for Evading the Royal Navy 75

Fact 68 - The Lost Treasure of La Buse 76

Fact 69 - Pirates and Their Extravagant Feasts 77

Fact 70 - The Role of Slaves in Pirates 78

Fact 71 - Pirates in the Red Sea 79

Fact 72 - The Pirates' Mysterious Maps 80

Fact 73 - The Secret Life of Black Sam Bellamy 81

Fact 74 - Techniques for navigating at night 82

Fact 75 - Pirates and Their Unexpected Alliances 83

Fact 76 - The Hidden Treasure of the Eastern Seas 84

Fact 77 - Pirates and Their Strange Beliefs 85

Fact 78 - The Secret of Sunken Wrecks 86

Fact 79 - Pirates and Their Amazing Remedies 87

Fact 80 - The Art of Piracy in the Mediterranean 88

Fact 81 - Pirates and Their Funny Hats 89

Fact 82 - Techniques for Taking a Fort 90

Fact 83 - The Pirate Oliver's Lost Treasure 91

Fact 84 - Pirates and Their Codes of Honor 92

Fact 85 - The Riddles of the Lost Islands 93

Fact 86 - The Mystery of the Pirates of the Caribbean 94

Fact 87 - Pirates and Their Funny Names 95

Fact 88 - Techniques for hoisting the sails 96

Fact 89 - Pirates and their adventures in Africa 97

Fact 90 - Henry Avery's Hidden Treasure 98

Fact 91 - Pirates and Their Amazing Customs 99

Fact 92 - The Secrets of Pirate Honeymoons 100

Fact 93 - Pirates and their unique coats of arms 101

Fact 94 - Techniques for Building a Ship 102

Fact 95 - Pirates and their incredible challenges 103
Fact 96 - The Lost Treasure of the Persian Gulf 104
Fact 97 - Pirates and their tricks to survive 105
Fact 98 - The Riddles of the Missing Ships 106
Fact 99 - Pirates and Their Incredible Legends 107
Fact 100 - The Art of Piracy Through the Ages 108
Conclusion 109
Quiz 110
Answers 116

"The stars guide the ships, but it's the stories of pirates and treasures that guide our dreams."

— Anthony T. Hincks

Introduction

Ahoy, adventurer of the seas of knowledge! If you hold this book in your hands, it's because you're thirsty for adventures, mysteries, and epic tales. And trust me, you won't be disappointed. Pirates, those legendary figures who have stood the test of time, have shaped maritime history far more than you could ever imagine. Every page you turn will immerse you in the fascinating world of piracy, with its codes, hidden treasures, epic battles and unsolved puzzles.

You will discover that reality often surpasses fiction. That behind every legend lies a true story, often even more incredible. From the Mediterranean of antiquity to the Caribbean of the 18th century, via the tumultuous seas of the North, you will sail through eras and oceans, alongside these daring men and women, who have chosen a life of freedom, sometimes at the cost of everything.

So, are you ready to set sail and embark on this epic adventure through the ages? Get on board with me and discover the 100 most incredible facts about pirates. Let the journey begin!

Marc Dresgui

Fact 1 - Blackbeard's Riddle

Ahoy Sailor! Have you ever heard of Blackbeard, one of the most feared pirates of all time? His real name was Edward Teach, and he haunted the seas in the early eighteenth century. With his long black beard and lighted locks that he placed under his hat, he looked like a demon straight out of hell. His reputation for cruelty was surpassed only by his ingenuity in piracy.

But do you know what's even more mysterious than his exploits? Its end! In 1718, Blackbeard was hunted down by Lieutenant Robert Maynard near North Carolina. After a fierce fight, Maynard managed to kill the famous pirate. But that's not all: when they examined his body, they discovered no less than five bullets and twenty cuts!

Blackbeard's ship, the "Queen Anne's Revenge", was found much later, in 1996. Thanks to this discovery, archaeologists and historians have been able to learn more about this legendary pirate. So, are you ready to dive into more pirate mysteries?

Fact 2 - Anne Bonny, the Terror of the Seas

Hello, young adventurer! Have you ever imagined a female pirate defying the seas and spreading terror among sailors? Let me introduce you to Anne Bonny, one of the most fearless pirates of the Golden Age of Piracy. Born in Ireland in 1700, she defied all the stereotypes of her time to become a Caribbean legend.

Anne was not only brave, she was also cunning. She often disguised herself as a man to better blend in with the crew of pirate ships. This ruse allowed him to surprise more than one enemy, who often underestimated the "lady" of the crew.

But what makes Anne truly memorable is her tumultuous relationship with another famous pirate, Calico Jack. Together, they formed a formidable duo, boldly attacking ships and sharing the spoils. But, like all great stories, their adventure ended tragically when their ship was captured in 1720.

Today, Anne Bonny remains a source of inspiration, reminding everyone that courage and determination have no gender. Ready for another adventure on the high seas?

Fact 3 — Why Pirates Wore Earrings

Hey, adventurer of the seas! Have you ever noticed that many pirates are often depicted with earrings? This might seem like a simple choice of style, but in reality, these ornaments often had a much deeper meaning.

For starters, many sailors believed that wearing a gold or silver earring could improve their eyesight! Amazing, isn't it? They believed that the metal had magical properties that could protect against blindness and other ailments. Who knows, maybe some pirates were just superstitious!

Then there was also a very practical reason: money. A gold or silver earring was considered a kind of insurance for a pirate. In the event of death, the sale of the earring could pay for a decent burial. A real treasure hanging from your ear, don't you think?

Finally, for some, it was also a sign of bravery or lived experiences, such as crossing the equator or surviving a shipwreck. So, the next time you see a pirate with an earring, you'll know there's a story behind that little piece of metal!

Fact 4 - The Mystery of the Hidden Treasures

Hello, young explorer! Who hasn't dreamed of discovering a hidden treasure? When we talk about pirates, we often think of those chests full of gold coins, buried in secret places. But do you really know why and how they hid their loot?

Most pirates buried their treasures to protect them. The seas were dangerous, and pirates weren't the only ones who wanted to steal the riches! By hiding their loot, they ensured that no one else could get their hands on it. A careful pirate was worth two, wasn't it?

But beware, not all pirates hid their treasures. Some spent their wealth as fast as they got it, in taverns, gambling, or merchandise. For them, life was a great adventure, and they wanted to make the most of it!

One of the most famous treasures is that of William Kidd, a pirate who is said to have hidden a huge booty near New York City. Even today, many adventurers are looking for this treasure. And you, would you be ready to embark on this quest to find out?

Fact 5 - The Secret Language of Pirates

Ahoy, curious sailor! Have you ever heard of the mysterious jargon of pirates? These scoundrels of the seas were not content with sailing and plundering; They also had their own language. Let's dive into this fascinating world of pirate communication.

First, it's important to understand that this language wasn't just for style. It served as a code so that other crews or enemies could not understand their conversations. For example, "Davy Jones" was a reference to the devil of the deep sea, and talking about "Davy Jones' Locker" meant that someone had died at sea.

However, their language was not just based on words. Hackers also used signals, flags, and symbols to communicate with each other at a distance. The famous black ensign adorned with a skull and crossed shins, the Jolly Roger, is one of the most recognizable symbols and signified that the approaching ship was a pirate ship.

The next time you read or hear a pirate story, pay attention to their language. You may be surprised to understand some of their secrets hidden in their words and symbols!

Fact 6 – The Strict Rules of Pirate Code

Did you know, dear adventurer, that pirates were not just lawless outlaws? Contrary to what you might think, they had a strict set of rules that they had to follow: pirate code. Let's immerse ourselves in these codes that governed life on the high seas.

These codes, often written down and accepted by the entire crew, defined the division of booty, conduct on board, and punishments for misconduct. For example, aboard Blackbeard's ship, it was strictly forbidden to play cards or dice. This kind of gambling could lead to arguments, debts and fights.

Treason or theft between crew members were serious offenses. According to some codes, if a pirate stole from another pirate, his punishment could be to be abandoned on a desert island. A fate far worse than simple hanging!

So, the next time you imagine pirates' lives as a never-ending adventure, remember that they also had rules to follow. Even on the high seas, order and discipline were essential for the survival of the crew.

Fact 7 - How Pirates Read the Stars

Have you ever looked up at the night sky, wondering how the navigators of yesteryear found their way through the vastness of the ocean? Pirates, those experts in navigation, were masters in the art of reading the stars.

The stars were essential for pirates. Without GPS or electronic compass, they depended on the starry sky to orient themselves. The North Star, for example, was crucial for those sailing in the Northern Hemisphere. It remains fixed and always points north, thus serving as a constant landmark in the night.

But it wasn't just the North Star. Constellations, such as Ursa Major or Orion, also played an important role. They changed their position according to the seasons, helping pirates understand where they were and what time of year.

So, the next time you look at the night sky, think about pirates and their adventures on the high seas. Thanks to the stars, they could cross oceans, find new lands, and hide their treasures in secret places.

Fact 8 - The True Face of Calico Jack

Calico Jack, whose real name is John Rackham, is a name that resonates in the history of piracy. But do you really know who this man was, behind the legends and epic tales?

Born in England in the early eighteenth century, Rackham was known for his penchant for colorful clothing, hence his nickname "Calico," a type of fabric. He was a pirate who preferred cunning to outright violence. Unlike other infamous pirates, he wasn't particularly known for his cruelty.

Perhaps the most intriguing aspect of his life is his relationship with two female pirates, Anne Bonny and Mary Read. Anne was his companion, while Mary had disguised herself as a man to join his crew. These two women, fighting alongside Calico Jack, overturned the stereotypes of the time about gender roles.

Calico Jack's end, however, was less glorious. Captured by the authorities in 1720, he was tried and hanged. But his legacy lives on, thanks to the tales of his exploits and his iconic flag: a skull with two crossed swords.

Fact 9 - Where does "Jolly Roger" come from?

The "Jolly Roger", with its iconic skull topped with two crossbones, is the flag most associated with pirates. But have you ever wondered where this name and this frightening image came from?

The exact origin of the term "Jolly Roger" remains mysterious, but it is probably derived from "pretty red" in French, which referred to the red flags hoisted by French pirates, announcing that no quarter would be given to their enemies. Over time, the term evolved and became anglicized.

The iconography of the skull and crossbones, on the other hand, is older than piracy itself. It has symbolized death since the Middle Ages. By adopting it, the hackers wanted to convey a clear message: "survive or die". In fact, there were many pirate flags, each with its own variation of the pattern.

The "Jolly Roger" is therefore a blend of cultures and histories, having evolved over time to become the universally recognized symbol of piracy, and a constant reminder of the danger posed by these outlaws of the seas.

Fact 10 - Pirates and their parrots

The image of a pirate with a parrot perched on his shoulder has become iconic. But do you know why these colorful birds were so prized by pirates?

Parrots, native to the tropics where many pirates sailed, were exotic and expensive animals at the time. Owning them was therefore a sign of wealth and success. Pirates would capture them during their stopovers and sell them at a good price once they returned to Europe. Some even kept these birds as pets, adding to their charisma and legend.

Beyond mere prestige, parrots played a social role aboard ships. With their ability to mimic the human voice, they entertained the crew on long sea voyages. Superstitious pirates even believed that these birds brought good luck.

Thus, between profit, companionship and superstition, parrots found their place alongside pirates, helping to forge an image that remains anchored in the collective imagination to this day.

Fact 11 - The Map That Leads to the Priceless

The treasure maps, marked with a cross where the loot is hidden, may seem like fiction to you. But these cards really did exist in the unforgiving world of piracy.

It's true that not all pirates created maps to hide their treasures, but a few did, especially if they wanted to bury a particularly valuable portion of their loot to retrieve later. The most famous example is that of Captain Kidd, who, according to legend, hid much of his wealth before being captured and executed.

However, these maps were not always reliable. In many cases, they were used as tricks to trick or set traps for other pirates or treasure hunters. In addition, the changing nature of the seascape often made cues and landmarks obsolete.

Thus, the quest for the hidden pirate treasure, guided by a mysterious map, remains one of the most seductive and enigmatic tales in the history of piracy, fueling legends and the collective imagination.

Fact 12 - The Courage of Mary Read, Pirate

When you think of pirates, bearded and rough men often come to mind. But Mary Read defied all those stereotypes. Raised as a boy by her mother, she embraced a male role for most of her life.

Mary didn't just disguise herself as a man to escape societal norms. She enlisted in the British Army and fought bravely. Later, she turned to piracy, where she met Anne Bonny, another renowned female pirate. Together, they spread terror in the Caribbean.

Although his life was short, his audacity left an indelible mark on the history of piracy. Captured and imprisoned, Mary died in prison, but her story lives on as a testament to one woman's determination and courage in a male-dominated world.

Whenever you hear about Mary Read, remember that she was a force to be reckoned with, demonstrating that courage and bravery have no gender.

Fact 13 - The Dance of Swords on the Bridge

Piracy was not just a matter of theft and plunder; It also involved skilled hand-to-hand combat. And when pirates engaged in combat, their weapon of choice was often the sword. The rattling of the waves on the deck of a ship was as common a sight as the hoisting of the pirate flag.

But did you know that these duels weren't always deadly? Sometimes they were organized to resolve internal conflicts or to prove the worth of a crew member. At the end of these battles, the victor was respected, and the vanquished, if he survived, was often forgiven and accepted back into the ranks.

The swords used by pirates were diverse: sabres, rapiers, and cutlasses. Each had its own technique and style. The cutlass, for example, was short and wide, ideal for close-quarters combat on the crowded decks of ships.

So, the next time you imagine pirates, think of that elegant and dangerous dance of swords, where every move counted, and mastery of the weapon could mean the difference between life and death.

Fact 14 - Did the pirates really eat cookies?

When you think of pirate food, you might imagine a feast of roasted meats and rum. However, the day-to-day reality was far less glamorous. Pirates, just like other sailors of the time, did eat "cookies," but not the ones you might think of.

These "biscuits" were actually sea bread or rusks, also called "hard biscuits". They were made to last a long time without spoiling, making them ideal for long sea voyages. However, their texture was so hard that they were often soaked in water or rum to soften them before being consumed.

The downside of these cookies was that they could harbor worms or weevils after a while. But that didn't necessarily discourage the pirates, because in harsh conditions, hunger took precedence over disgust.

So, even though fictionalized stories often feature pirates feasting and drinking, don't forget that hard, simple, and often infested little cookie, which was actually an essential part of their diet.

Fact 15 - How to avoid seasickness

If you think the pirate life was always an exciting adventure, think again. Even the most hardened of pirates could suffer from seasickness. This inconvenience, caused by the movement of the boat, can cause feelings of dizziness, nausea and even vomiting.

Hackers were using a variety of methods to counter this malaise. For example, staring at the horizon or a fixed point in the distance helped to reduce the sensation of movement. This trick is still used today by many people traveling by sea.

Eating light foods, avoiding alcohol, and staying in the fresh air were other popular tricks among hackers. Some also believed in the effectiveness of sea bracelets, which were believed to exert pressure on certain points on the wrist to reduce nausea.

So, the next time you find yourself at sea and start to feel a little nauseous, remember the tricks of those old sea dogs. After all, if they worked for them, they might work for you too!

Fact 16 - The Secrets of the Ghost Ships

Ghost ships have always been among the most haunting legends of the seas. Imagine a ship, soulless on board, sailing eternally, lost in the vast ocean. These stories give you chills, don't you? But where do these myths come from?

One of the most famous ghost ships is the "Flying Dutchman". Legend has it that he was cursed to sail forever, unable to land. Sailors claim to have seen it, often illuminated by a strange light, portending misfortune for those who cross its path.

Some of these legends may have originated in real ships found adrift, with a missing or dead crew. The causes vary: epidemics, mutinies, or extreme weather conditions. The lack of a clear explanation has often fueled speculation and terrifying stories.

The sea is vast and mysterious, and even in pirate times, it kept many secrets. So, are ghost ships really the result of curses or just unsolved riddles of the sea? Maybe we'll never really know.

Fact 17 - Pirates and Their Mystical Tattoos

Pirates are often associated with images of skulls and crossbones, but did you know that many of them also sport meaningful tattoos? These marks inked on their skin were not just decorations, they had a deep meaning for those who wore them.

A common tattoo among pirates was that of the mermaid or turtle, a symbol of respect for the sea and belief in its protection. Some believed that these creatures would guide them safely through the rushing waters or protect them from drowning.

Stars, anchors, or birds, such as swallows, were also popular motifs. A swallow, for example, often represented the hope of always finding its way home, as this bird is known for its incredible migration abilities.

So, the next time you see a pirate depicted with a tattoo, take a moment to think about what it might mean. These images are not just simple drawings; They tell stories of adventures, beliefs and hopes.

Fact 18 - Turtle Island, the Privateers' Lair

Have you ever heard of Turtle Island? Located off the northwest coast of Haiti, this island has played a major role in the history of piracy. In the 17th century, it was the undisputed haunt of pirates and privateers, becoming one of the most feared bases in the Caribbean.

The island's strategic position, away from the main sea routes, made it an ideal place for pirates. There they could repair their ships, refuel, and plan their next attacks away from the prying eyes of European navies. Pirates such as Henry Morgan used this base to launch devastating raids on Spanish settlements.

In addition to its strategic importance, Turtle Island was also a crossroads of cultures. Pirates of all origins rubbed shoulders, exchanging stories, techniques, and loot. The atmosphere was so unique that it inspired many tales and legends.

So, the next time you're sailing through the waters of the Caribbean, imagine the shadows of the famous privateers who once dominated these waters from their island fortress.

Fact 19 - Who were the Buccaneers?

Did you know that pirates are not the only ones who have left their mark on the maritime history of the Caribbean? Buccaneers were also very influential, but they had a very different origin. They get their name from the word "boucan," a Native American method of smoking meat on a wooden frame.

Originally, buccaneers were hunters, mainly of pigs and cows, on the island of Hispaniola. They smoked the meat to preserve it and sell it to passing sailors. However, after being hunted by the Spanish, these hunters turned to piracy, using their navigational and hunting skills to attack ships.

By combining their intimate knowledge of the area with their hunting skills, buccaneers quickly became fearsome pirates. They were particularly adept at boarding, using muskets with deadly accuracy.

So, when you think of piracy, don't forget those hunters-turned-pirates. Buccaneers left an indelible mark on the tumultuous world of the 17th century Caribbean.

Fact 20 - A Pirate Foamer's Life

Have you ever wondered what it's like to be the youngest aboard a pirate ship? The moss, often a young boy, occupied this position. Although he may have dreamed of adventures at sea, the reality was often quite different from his fantasies.

The life of a moss was not easy. He was responsible for the most menial tasks, such as cleaning the deck, serving meals, and assisting with the manoeuvring of the ship. Despite his young age, he had to work hard, and often without recognition or gratitude from the crew.

But there were also benefits. By being in daily contact with seasoned pirates, the moss learned the tricks of the trade, from navigation techniques to combat skills. Some mosses, in time, became skilled pirates or even feared captains.

So, despite the challenges and dangers, the life of moss offered a unique opportunity for learning and upward mobility in the unforgiving world of pirates. A boy of today could well be the captain of tomorrow.

Fact 21 - The Mysterious Pirate Lady of China

Have you ever heard of Ching Shih, one of the most powerful pirates in history? This impressive woman dominated the China Seas in the early 19th century, even defying China's mighty imperial fleet.

Originally from Guangzhou, Ching Shih began his career as a simple prostitute. However, after marrying the dreaded pirate Cheng I, she quickly took control of the fleet upon his death. With an armada of more than 1,500 ships and 80,000 men under its command, it imposed its strict rules, guaranteeing the discipline and loyalty of its troops.

Not content with its maritime dominance, it skillfully negotiated with the Chinese government to secure an amnesty for its men. This allowed him to retire peacefully, keeping his accumulated wealth, and spend the rest of his life running a brothel and casino.

This female pirate, endowed with unprecedented intelligence and audacity, is a shining testament to what determination and courage can accomplish, even in a male-dominated world.

Fact 22 - Captain Kidd's Lost Treasure

Have you ever wondered if stories of hidden treasures are true? The story of Captain William Kidd is one of the most famous about a pirate treasure that has not yet been found. Kidd, contrary to popular belief, began his career as a pirate hunter, employed to protect ships from threats from the sea.

However, there was a fine line between pirate and pirate hunter at the time. Accused of piracy, Kidd returned to New York in hopes of proving his innocence. Before doing so, he hid some of his treasure on Gardiners Island, hoping to use it later for his defense.

Unfortunately for Kidd, he was arrested, tried, and hanged in 1701 in London. The part of the treasure he had hidden on Gardiners Island has been found, but rumor has it that he had amassed much greater riches, hidden elsewhere, that have never been discovered.

So, whenever you hear a story about a treasure map or treasure hunt, remember Captain Kidd and the lingering mystery of his lost treasure. Who knows, maybe you'll be the adventurer who will discover it one day?

Fact 23 - Techniques for Spotting a Ship

Do you realize that before modern technology, pirates had their own tricks to spot ships on the horizon? Their methods, though archaic, were surprisingly effective.

First, they used the lookout. It was often the youngest and most agile crew member, perched in the crow's nest at the top of the main mast. Thanks to its elevated position, it could see beyond the curvature of the earth, spotting sails or smoke from impressive distances. A cry of "Ship in sight!" from the lookout often announced adventure or danger.

In addition, the pirates watched the birds. Birds flying in a circle could indicate a ship below, especially if they were far from land. The movements of fish and other marine animals could also betray the presence of a nearby ship.

So, the next time you imagine a pirate scanning the horizon with a spotting scope, remember that he also had other techniques, in harmony with nature, to detect his next target. These cunning sailors knew how to use their surroundings to their advantage.

Fact 24 - How Pirates Avoided Sharks

Did you know that the waters in which pirates sailed were often infested with sharks? These predators were a real threat to anyone who fell overboard or had to swim from place to place. However, the cunning and cunning pirates had their own strategies to avoid these terrifying creatures.

First, they avoided throwing food scraps overboard, as this could attract sharks. If a shark was spotted nearby, a break was made in all water activities, including deck cleaning, to avoid attracting the animal's attention.

Pirates also used drums or beat the side of the ship to scare away sharks. These loud, vibrating noises were unpleasant for sharks, which prefer to approach their prey discreetly.

Finally, when necessary, they would sometimes throw a piece of meat away from the ship to distract the shark and steer it in the opposite direction. Thanks to these techniques, many pirates have managed to escape the sharp jaws of these fearsome predators.

Fact 25 - Pirates' Favorite Musical Instruments

Did you know that music was an essential part of life aboard a pirate ship? It was used to maintain crew morale, pace tasks and entertain during long hours at sea. Each instrument had its own importance and was chosen for its unique sound and practicality on board.

The accordion was one of the most popular instruments. Easy to carry and capable of producing a loud, melodious sound, it was often used to accompany singing and dancing. Hearing this instrument, you could be sure that a party was going on on the deck.

The drum, on the other hand, served a double purpose. It marked the rhythm of songs, but was also used to set the tempo for tasks such as hoisting sails or cleaning the deck. He was the bosco's instrument of choice.

Finally, the flute and fiddle were also popular, bringing a sweet, melancholic melody to calm nights at sea. With these instruments, pirates turned their harsh and dangerous lives into a melodious adventure.

Fact 26 - The surprising role of cats on board

Have you ever imagined cats wandering on the decks of a pirate ship, between cannons and treasure chests? These felines weren't just there for company. They had a far more crucial mission aboard ships.

The main reason for the cats' presence was pest control. The ships, with their food supplies and dark, damp areas, were a haven for rats. These rodents could damage supplies, gnaw on ropes, and spread disease. Cats, with their natural hunting instincts, were excellent rat exterminators.

In addition to their role as hunters, cats were also considered good luck charms. Sailors believed that these felines could bring good luck on sea voyages and protect the ship from evil spirits.

However, despite their usefulness, these cats had to adapt to life on the high seas, just like their human companions. Thanks to them, life on board was healthier, and maybe even a little sweeter with their soothing purrs.

Fact 27 - The Amazing Friendship Between Pirates and Turtles

Do you know the strange relationship between pirates and sea turtles? At first glance, you might think that a hardy pirate and a slow turtle would have nothing in common. Yet, their interaction is fascinating.

Turtles, despite their peaceful appearance, were a valuable source of food for pirates on their long sea voyages. The Caribbean islands, frequented by many pirates, were home to turtle colonies. These animals were easy to capture when they came to lay their eggs on the beaches.

But turtles weren't just hunted for their meat. Their shells, once polished and worked, could be transformed into precious objects, such as combs, glasses or boxes. These items were often sold or traded in ports, adding another source of income for pirates.

But beyond these practical uses, some legends speak of pirates forming affectionate bonds with these creatures, keeping them as pets or releasing them after capturing them. After all, the sea has many surprises in store, even between the most unlikely of friends.

Fact 28 - Secret Codes on Cards

Have you ever wondered how pirates manage to hide the location of their treasures? If you think it was just a cross on a map, you're a long way from the complex reality of pirate cards.

Hackers were actually using codes and symbols to hide essential information on their cards. Rather than simply marking "X" for the location of the treasure, they used specific icons to indicate hazards, traps, or natural landmarks. Some of them had even developed coded language, understandable only by themselves and their close allies.

In addition, the maps were often intentionally wrong. Pirates would add fictitious islands or alter distances to fool those who might stumble upon these maps. That way, even if someone found their card, they would be directed to a red herring.

Finally, confidence was rare among these sea robbers. Some pirates preferred to keep the exact location of the treasure in their heads, using the map only as a tool for distraction or negotiation. Thus, pirate treasures remain one of the greatest mysteries of the oceans to this day.

Fact 29 - Techniques to avoid capture

Pirates, masters of the sea, were not only skilled at attacking, but also at escaping from those who chased them. You're probably wondering how they managed to elude capture for years? The answer lies in a combination of cunning, strategy and, sometimes, sheer luck.

First, pirates often changed the appearance of their ships. By quickly changing sails or masking distinguishing markings, they made their boat unrecognizable. For example, the famous pirate Blackbeard has been known to cover his ship's lanterns with a thick cloth to navigate in the dark and escape the sight of enemy ships.

Secondly, pirates knew the waters better than anyone. They used narrow passages and shallow areas, inaccessible to larger ships, to escape when pursued. They knew every cove and hiding place, and used that knowledge to their advantage.

Finally, the hackers knew how to use the elements to their advantage. By carefully studying ocean currents and weather conditions, they could predict the best time to sail or hide, leaving their pursuers far behind.

Fact 30 - Were the Pirates Really Lawless?

The image of the cruel, unscrupulous pirate roaming the seven seas in search of loot is ingrained in popular culture. But did you know that this image is only partially true? In reality, most pirate crews were governed by strict codes, guaranteeing some form of order on board.

These codes of conduct, often referred to as "articles of piracy", set out specific rules on the division of booty, conduct at sea, and the treatment of prisoners. For example, in Bartholomew Roberts' crew, it was strictly forbidden to play cards or make noise after sunset.

Also, contrary to popular belief, many pirates were very superstitious. They had their own beliefs and rituals to attract good luck or appease the spirits of the seas. Wearing gold earrings was, for some, a way to provide protection against drowning.

In conclusion, although pirates lived on the margins of society, they were not necessarily chaotic or lawless. In reality, their world had its own order and rules, sometimes even stricter than those of legitimate sailors.

Fact 31 - The Mystery of the Wooden Legs

When the image of a pirate is conjured up, one of the first things that comes to mind is that of a man with an eye patch, a parrot on his shoulder and, of course, a wooden leg. But have you ever wondered where this specific representation came from?

Life at sea was dangerous, and it was not uncommon for sailors to suffer serious injuries, even leading to amputations. Wooden legs were therefore used as prostheses by some sailors to replace a lost limb. However, the reality of these prostheses was far from fiction. Rather than elaborate, artistically sculpted legs, most were rudimentary, made to be functional.

Perhaps the most famous example is the pirate Long John Silver from Robert Louis Stevenson's novel "Treasure Island." This fictional character has greatly contributed to anchoring the image of the lame pirate in the collective imagination.

In short, although some pirates did indeed wear wooden legs, the reality was often less romantic and more practical than tales and legends would have us believe.

Fact 32 - The Legends of Sir Francis Drake

You've probably heard of Sir Francis Drake, one of the most famous pirates in history. But did you know that he was also an eminent navigator, explorer and vice-admiral in the English Navy?

Drake made the second solo circumnavigation of the globe between 1577 and 1580, a remarkable feat for the time. During this expedition, he attacked and plundered several Spanish ships, earning him the reputation of a fearsome pirate in the eyes of the Spanish. In England, on the other hand, he was considered a national hero, having greatly enriched the country's coffers through his catches.

Perhaps his most famous feat was his victory over the Invincible Spanish Armada in 1588. Although he was only one of the commanders of the English fleet, his shrewd tactics and knowledge of the seas played a crucial role in the rout of the Spanish.

Thus, Sir Francis Drake is a perfect example of the fine line between pirate and hero. Depending on one's point of view, he can be seen as a scourge of the seas or as a daring defender of the English crown.

Fact 33 - The Compass, Pirates' Precious Friend

Do you realize how crucial navigational instruments were to pirates? The compass, in particular, was their most valuable ally. Without it, navigating the vast expanses of the ocean would have been nearly impossible.

As soon as it appeared in Europe around the 12th century, the compass revolutionized navigation. Pirates, in particular, adopted it to orient themselves at sea and continue their quests for treasure. Before its invention, they had to rely on less reliable methods like stargazing, which wasn't always possible.

In addition to orientation, the compass allowed them to accurately map sea routes, secret hiding places, and treasure locations. For example, the famous pirate Edward "Blackbeard" Teach was known to have a set of state-of-the-art navigational instruments, including a compass, allowing him to evade his pursuers and find hidden treasures.

Thus, far from being simple bandits of the seas, pirates were shrewd navigators. Using tools like the compass, they were able to explore, conquer, and hide their loot with astonishing precision.

Fact 34 - Alliances between pirates and natives

Have you ever imagined pirates making alliances with natives on their travels? It may seem surprising, but these alliances were actually quite common and mutually beneficial.

Pirates, upon landing on uncharted lands, often needed resources, local information, and sometimes shelter to hide or repair their ships. The indigenous peoples, who knew their territory perfectly, were valuable allies in these needs. In exchange, pirates could offer goods, weapons, or even their help in local conflicts.

For example, the famous pirate William Dampier formed relationships with the Pacific natives during his travels. These alliances have allowed it to collect information on shipping routes, currents, and natural resources.

These associations, however, were not without tension. Sometimes, mistrust or misunderstandings led to confrontations. But, in many cases, cooperation between pirates and natives was a shrewd way for both sides to make the best of their respective situations.

Fact 35 - Blackbeard's True Loot

Do you remember the most infamous pirate of all time, Blackbeard? Despite its terrifying image and flamboyant legends, do you know what really made up its treasure?

The majority of Blackbeard's loot did not consist of gold or precious stones, as one might think. In reality, it was more about goods like sugar, cocoa or tobacco, which were very valuable at the time. These goods could be sold or traded, offering the pirate an immense fortune.

One of Blackbeard's most famous prizes was the French ship "La Concorde", which he renamed "Queen Anne's Revenge". This ship did not contain chests full of gold, but its value lay in its potential as a warship, fast and well armed.

However, this does not mean that Blackbeard has never got his hands on gold or jewels. But, in general, his real treasure lay in the goods and ships themselves, which enabled him to extend his dominion and influence over the seas.

Fact 36 - Amulets to protect against storms

When you're navigating the vast expanse of oceans, storms are one of the most unpredictable and frightening threats. Have you ever imagined how pirates, those daring sailors, sought to protect themselves from the wrath of nature?

Many pirates, despite their reputation as tough guys, were very superstitious. They believed in the power of amulets to protect them on their travels. These talismans, often made of bones, stones, or fragments of wood, were believed to deflect bad fortune and appease the spirits of the sea.

A famous example is the Eye of Saint Lucia amulet, a small spiral shell, which was thought to have the power to protect its wearer from storms. Many pirates wore this amulet around their necks, hoping that its presence would guide them through the rough seas.

So, the next time you hear about pirates braving the tumultuous oceans, don't forget those little items they held so preciously, hoping they would offer them protection and luck in their perilous adventures.

Fact 37 - Pirates and Seabirds

Did you know that pirates often share their marine world with seabirds? These aerial creatures were not only passenger companions for sailors, but also had strategic importance.

Seabirds, especially albatrosses and seagulls, were often observed by pirates as signs of nearby land. This is because these birds usually don't stray too far from the coast. When pirates spotted a group of seabirds in the middle of the ocean, they knew that a land or island was not far away.

But there was more to it than that. Some pirates believed that these birds were the souls of missing sailors, and killing them was considered a bad omen. For example, the legendary pirate John Silver was known to have a parrot on his shoulder, reflecting the close connection between these sea marauders and birds.

So, the next time you think of pirates, don't forget the seabirds that flew above them, playing a far more significant role than you could ever imagine.

Fact 38 - The Great Pirate Prison Escape

Have you ever wondered how a captured pirate could escape the clutches of his captors? One of the most daring escapes in the history of piracy occurred at the infamous Port Royal Prison.

Port Royal Prison, located in Jamaica, was notorious for its appalling conditions and ruthless guards. But in 1686, a pirate named Henry Every, with the help of a few of his companions, hatched a bold plan. Using stolen tools and their knowledge of the tides, they dug a tunnel under the prison walls for several nights.

Once the tunnel was completed, Every and his team chose a moonless night for their escape. They managed to outwit the guards and reach a small boat they had hidden nearby. Silently navigating through the dark waters, they finally regained freedom.

This spectacular escape became legendary among pirates, showing that even in the most desperate situations, with ingenuity and determination, a pirate could always find a way to escape.

Fact 39 - Secret Signals Between Pirate Ships

Have you ever imagined how pirates communicate discreetly on the high seas, away from prying ears? Secret signals were key to their coordination at sea, especially when they had to avoid revealing their intentions.

Pavilions were one of their favorite ways. By hoisting a certain type of flag or changing its position, a pirate ship could transmit messages to another ship from a distance. For example, a red flag often meant "no quarter," indicating that they would not take prisoners.

In addition, the hackers also used light signals at night. With lanterns placed in certain places on the ship or by using specific light codes, they could send information without being detected by enemy ships.

But it wasn't always necessary to use visible signals. Sometimes coded cannon shots or sequences of pirate songs were used to convey messages. These methods, combined with their audacity and cunning, made the pirates masters of the seas and always one step ahead of their opponents.

Fact 40 - Strange Animals on Board Ships

When you think of a pirate ship, you might picture a rough crew and chests full of gold. But did you know that these ships were also often home to strange and exotic animals?

Pirates, on their many journeys, stumbled upon fascinating creatures unknown to their homeland. For example, while sailing in the waters of the Indian Ocean, it was not uncommon for them to capture brightly colored parrots, which they brought back as pets or to sell them at a high price. These birds were not only aesthetically pleasing, their ability to mimic the human voice was highly valued.

Aside from parrots, some pirates had a soft spot for more exotic creatures like monkeys and lemurs. These little beasts, with their curious mannerisms and nimble movements, were often a source of entertainment on board.

But these animals weren't always just mascots. Some were used to intimidate enemies, while others, such as cats, had a utilitarian role in hunting rats. Thus, life aboard a pirate ship was an astonishing mix of human and animal adventure.

Fact 41 - The Secret Recipe for Pirate Rum

Ah, rum! This amber drink is often associated with pirates, and for good reason. Rum was an essential part of pirate life. But did you know that these buccaneers had their own secret recipe for concocting this drink?

The base of rum is fermented molasses, a by-product of making sugar. Once distilled, the base drink can be quite brutal. Still, the hackers had their own tricks to soften it. For example, some added spices like cinnamon, nutmeg, and cloves to give character to the liquid.

In addition to spices, pirates sometimes liked to mix rum with lemon or lime juice to combat scurvy, a disease caused by vitamin C deficiency. This mixture, nicknamed "grog", was not only tasty but also beneficial to health.

So, the next time you're enjoying a glass of rum, think of pirates and their culinary ingenuity. They not only knew how to navigate the seas, but also how to make a drink that stands the test of time!

Fact 42 - Pirates in the Panama Canal

You probably learned it in school: the Panama Canal is this incredible waterway that connects the Atlantic Ocean to the Pacific Ocean. But before it was built, did you know that this area was a real hideout for pirates?

In the 17th century, the Isthmus of Panama region was an essential route for the Spanish. They transported gold and silver from South America to Spain by crossing the isthmus on foot and then loading the treasures onto ships in the Caribbean Sea. This wealth had not gone unnoticed by the pirates.

Privateers like the famous Henry Morgan launched attacks on cities like Panama Viejo, taking advantage of the vulnerable territory. In 1671, Morgan and his men managed to plunder and burn the city, leaving with a huge booty.

These pirate incursions eventually influenced geopolitical decisions, pushing for the construction of the canal in the 20th century. So, whenever you hear about the Panama Canal, remember the daring pirates who once prowled its waters!

Fact 43 - The Art of Negotiation in Pirates

Contrary to popular belief, the pirate life was not just about violent looting and savage boardings. You'd be surprised to learn that these buccaneers of the seas were also skilled negotiators.

The pirates knew the importance of hostage-taking. For example, when they captured a ship, rather than destroying everything, they could hold the captain or crew in exchange for ransom. Bartholomew Roberts, a renowned pirate, often used this technique to increase his fortune without bloodshed.

It was also not uncommon to see pirates negotiating with each other to share the spoils, avoid conflicts, or even form alliances. "Articles of piracy" were sometimes established to ensure a fair distribution of treasures.

So, the next time you imagine a pirate, think also of a cunning strategist, able to skillfully haggle to maximize his gains while minimizing risk. Their success depended not only on their strength, but also on their ability to negotiate.

Fact 44 - Pirate Remedies for Scurvy

Scurvy, the terrible disease caused by vitamin C deficiency, was the haunt of all sailors, including pirates. You can imagine how difficult it is to maintain a balanced diet when you spend months at sea. The symptoms, including fatigue, joint pain, and bleeding gums, were dreadful and could decimate a crew.

Pirates, despite their badass image, were also potential victims. Some captains, more enlightened than others, understood the importance of carrying citrus fruits, such as lemons and oranges, known for their vitamin C content. For example, the notorious pirate Edward Teach, better known as Blackbeard, insisted on having supplies of these fruits on board.

Others, on the other hand, stumbled upon remedies. The consumption of local fish or exotic fruits during stopovers could sometimes provide enough vitamin C to prevent the disease.

So, even though piracy was a life full of dangers, it also had its moments of light, where cunning and knowledge could make all the difference between life and death.

Fact 45 - The Role of Women in the Golden Age

When you think of pirates, you may picture rough, bearded men, but did you know that some of the most notorious figures of the golden age of piracy were women? Despite a male-dominated era, some women have managed to carve out a place for themselves in this unforgiving world.

Take Anne Bonny and Mary Read, for example, two female pirates whose tales of bravery and daring are legendary. Disguised as men, they sailed across the seas, fighting on par with their male counterparts. These women were not only present for the parade, they were real actors in the looting and fighting.

Another interesting fact was that some women used piracy as a way to escape a life of social restrictions and misery. The ocean offered a promise of freedom, adventure, and equality that they couldn't find on land.

Thus, even though they were fewer in number, women from the golden age of piracy played a crucial role, proving once again that the sea knows no gender.

Fact 46 - Pirates and Their Amazing Jewels

You've probably seen images of pirates proudly sporting gold earrings and sparkling necklaces. But do you know why these scoundrels were so attracted to jewels? There was much more behind this fascination than just a taste for bling-bling.

Gold earrings, for example, weren't just a sign of wealth. According to some beliefs, they had the ability to protect or improve eyesight. In addition, in the event of death in a faraway location, the sale of these earrings could fund a dignified funeral for the deceased pirate.

The jewelry also served as a "portable bank." In a world where pirates were constantly on the move and betrayal was common, turning one's wealth into jewelry was a clever way to secure one's loot.

But, make no mistake, these ornaments were also the expression of a pronounced taste for extravagance. A richly decked pirate was often respected and feared, his appearance reflecting his success in the trade. Jewelry, for these outlaws, was at once utility, protection, and status symbol.

Fact 47 - The First Female Pirate Captain

You might think that the ruthless world of piracy was reserved exclusively for men. Think again! Women also played key roles in this world, and some of them were even feared. Let me tell you the story of the first woman to become a pirate captain.

Ching Shih, a Chinese woman, is this amazing woman. Originally, she worked in a brothel before marrying Cheng I, a feared pirate. After his death, far from retiring, she took control of his fleet, which consisted of hundreds of ships and tens of thousands of pirates. Its leadership was so strong that even the Chinese Empire struggled to fight it.

Under his leadership, strict codes were established to maintain discipline among his men. These rules included clear guidelines on how to divide the loot and how to treat prisoners, especially women.

Ching Shih was not just a woman in a man's world, she was a force to be reckoned with. She eventually retired with an official pardon and lived the rest of her life peacefully, a rarity for pirates of her caliber.

Fact 48 - The World's Most Wanted Treasures

Stories of buried treasures have always excited the imagination. Imagine chests filled with gold coins, glittering jewels, and precious artifacts, hidden somewhere, just waiting to be discovered. Pirates have often been associated with these mythical treasures, and some remain elusive to this day.

The treasure of the Spanish fleet of 1715 is an example of this. After a devastating hurricane, eleven of the twelve ships loaded with gold, silver, and precious stones that were en route to Spain sank off the coast of Florida. Although many artifacts have been recovered, it is said that much of the treasure is still underwater.

There's also Captain Kidd's enigmatic treasure. This British pirate buried some of his loot on Gardiners Island in New York. However, rumors persist that he may have hidden other treasures elsewhere, but these have never been found.

Every undiscovered treasure becomes a legend, attracting treasure hunters from all over the world. Who knows, maybe one day you'll go in search of one of these lost treasures?

Fact 49 - Life Aboard a Ship in Combat

Have you ever imagined the adrenaline rushing through a pirate's body during a fight at sea? Life aboard a pirate ship in combat was tumultuous, intense, and often brutal. When the cannonballs began to fly, each member of the crew had a specific role to play.

During an attack, gunners would rush to load and fire the cannons, creating a deafening symphony of detonations and smoke. The projectiles whistled through the air, damaging the sails and wood, while shrapnel scraped or wounded the men. As an example, the notorious pirate Black Bart was known to orchestrate over 400 attacks, and each assault was a coordinated spectacle of chaos.

On deck, the pirates armed themselves with swords, pistols, and muskets, ready to board the enemy ship. Boarding was a close-quarters combat event, where pirates had to show their courage and skill in battle.

Despite the ever-present danger, these battles were the essence of pirate life. The risk was enormous, but the potential loot and fame that could be gained by emerging victorious was often worth it.

Fact 50 - Privateers, Heroes or Pirates

Did you know that there is a fine line between being a pirate and a privateer? Privateers were like pirates, but with one important nuance: they operated with the approval of their government. Armed with "letters of marque", they were authorized to attack the ships of enemy countries.

Where pirates hunted for their own profit, privateers were an unofficial extension of a country's navy. For example, the famous Sir Francis Drake, although considered a hero in England, was seen as a pirate by the Spanish. To the English, his exploits enriched the crown, while to the Spaniards he was nothing more than a thief of the seas.

Nevertheless, life aboard a privateer ship was not much different from that of a pirate ship. Fighting, boarding, and searching for treasure were part of their daily lives.

In the end, the distinction between privateer and pirate often depended on perspective. To some, they were national heroes, defending the interests of their homeland, but to others, they were just brigands of the seas.

Fact 51 - How Pirates Hid Their Loot

You've probably heard of hidden treasures, buried on deserted islands, waiting to be discovered. But do you really know how the pirates hid their precious loot? It was an art in itself.

Contrary to popular belief, not all pirates hid their gold and jewels when they buried them. Many preferred to invest in tangible goods or exchange their loot for goods. However, those who chose to bury their riches did so with great caution. They chose remote locations, away from prying eyes, and discreetly marked the location so they could return.

It is important to note that many of these hidden treasures have never been found. Sometimes the pirate who hid the treasure would die before they could retrieve it, or the natural landmarks they used to identify the location would change over time.

The quest for these lost treasures has fascinated many adventurers throughout the centuries. But don't forget: if the idea of finding hidden treasure appeals to you, pirate treasure maps are often misleading and full of puzzles!

Fact 52 - The Mysteries of the South Seas

The South Seas have always been shrouded in mystery and fascination. For those of you who dream of adventure, imagine sailing on these turquoise waters, where the pirates of yesteryear sought fortune and glory.

These seas were the playground of many famous pirates, such as William Dampier, who explored Australia long before James Cook. Dampier, both pirate and explorer, left behind detailed accounts of his voyages, revealing the beauties and dangers of the South Seas.

But it wasn't just beauty that attracted pirates. The South Seas were renowned for their lucrative trade routes, especially the spice trade. Islands like the Moluccas were nicknamed "the Spice Islands" because they were the main source of nutmeg, cloves, and other valuable spices.

However, these seas were also fraught with dangers. In addition to storms and treacherous reefs, pirates often had to contend with indigenous peoples who protected their lands. These challenges, however, have not deterred pirates from seeking their fortunes in these mysterious waters. Who knows what treasure is yet to be discovered there?

Fact 53 - Technique for Boarding a Ship

When you picture pirates in action, you probably think of hectic scenes of boarding. But did you know that the art of boarding a ship is a science in itself, requiring strategy and finesse?

First of all, discretion was crucial. Pirates, such as the notorious Black Bart Roberts, often used deceptively peaceful sails to approach their targets without arousing suspicion. Once close enough, they hoisted the black flag, sowing terror among the opposing crew.

The element of surprise was key. Some pirates, such as Calico Jack, were experts at using grappling hooks to silently get close to their prey. Once the grappling hooks were launched and anchored, the pirates would pull on the ropes, bringing the two ships closer together to facilitate the assault.

Finally, the hand-to-hand combat began. Armed with swords, pistols, and daggers, pirates invaded the ship, seeking to gain control as quickly as possible. This combination of cunning, surprise, and bravery made pirates formidable adversaries on the seas.

Fact 54 - Pirates and their board games

You might think that pirates spent all their time raiding or sailing the seas. Yet, like any good sailor, they needed distractions on their long crossings. Board games were a great way to pass the time and bond between the crew.

Dice were especially popular aboard pirate ships. With simple rules and requiring little hardware, the dice game has been a favorite among pirates such as Blackbeard. Often, these games were accompanied by bets, thus increasing the tension and excitement.

Another popular game was tic-tac-toe, traced on the deck of the ship or on a piece of paper. Simplicity and strategy were mixed in this ancestral game, allowing two players to challenge each other intellectually without the need for an elaborate board.

Finally, chess and checkers were also popular games for those lucky enough to have a board. These games, which required thought and tactics, showed that, contrary to popular belief, pirates were not just brutes, but individuals capable of finesse and strategy.

Fact 55 - Buccaneers' Favorite Songs

Imagine yourself aboard a pirate ship, with the wind blowing and the waves crashing. In addition to the sound of the sea, another melody comes to you: that of the songs sung by the buccaneers. Music has always been an essential part of sailors' lives, and pirates were no exception.

One of the most popular songs was "Drunken Sailor". Originally, it was a work song, used to synchronize efforts during tasks such as hoisting a sail. But over time, it became a hymn of joy and carefreeness, taken up at the top of its lungs during the festivities on board.

There were also ballads that told stories of love, adventure, and betrayal. For example, "Maid of Amsterdam" is a song about a sailor's love for a woman he left behind. These ballads touched the hearts of the pirates, reminding them of their humanity and memories of home.

Finally, we must not forget the songs that celebrated victories or told of the exploits of famous pirates. Through these melodies, legends lived on and inspired new generations of buccaneers to take to the sea.

Fact 56 - Pirates and Voodoo Magic

Have you ever wondered, dear reader, what are the supernatural beliefs of pirates? Voodoo magic and pirates are more intimately linked than you might think. The Caribbean, the birthplace of voodoo and the epicenter of the Golden Age of Piracy, was a place where superstitions and beliefs in supernatural forces were omnipresent.

Many pirates strongly believed that certain people had the power to summon spirits or cast spells. For example, the notorious pirate Blackbeard was reputed to light flaming fuses in his beard to appear more terrifying, fueling rumors that he had supernatural powers.

Amulets and talismans were commonly used aboard pirate ships, as they were believed to offer protection and good luck. Some pirates even resorted to voodoo priests to bless their expeditions or curse their enemies.

However, it is important to note that not all pirates believed in or practiced voodoo. But voodoo culture and beliefs certainly influenced the life and legends of the Caribbean Sea during these tumultuous times.

Fact 57 - The Invention of Treasure Maps

Have you ever wondered, dear reader, where did those treasure maps marked with a cross, often seen in movies and stories about pirates, come from? The idea of maps leading to hidden treasures is deeply ingrained in our popular culture, but where do they really come from?

Historically, the first mentions of treasure maps don't really date back to the golden age of piracy. Instead, they appear primarily in 19th-century literature and adventure stories. These works shaped our perception of pirates and contributed to the romantic idea of epic treasure hunts.

There have been a few real-life cases of pirates, such as William Kidd, who have left clues or indications of the location of their loot. However, the notion that they regularly drew detailed maps, marked with a cross to indicate the treasure, is more myth than reality.

It is therefore important to distinguish between fiction and reality. While the idea of treasure maps is appealing, they are more a figment of our collective imagination than a common practice among hackers of old.

Fact 58 - Pirates' Navigational Instruments

Navigating the vast expanses of water, dear reader, was not an easy task, especially in the age of pirates. Without GPS or modern technology, how did they find their way on the high seas?

The compass was an essential instrument. Although it existed long before the golden age of piracy, this tool was fundamental to determining direction. By observing the pointing of the needle to magnetic north, the pirates could set their course. The astrolabe, another fascinating tool, was used to measure the altitude of stars and planets, allowing navigators to deduce their latitude.

The sextant, although it became more common after the golden age of piracy, was also a valuable tool. It was used to measure the angle between an astral object and the horizon. Coupled with navigation tables, it helped to determine the position at sea with remarkable accuracy.

But, don't be fooled! Navigation was a complex art, requiring great expertise. These instruments, combined with knowledge of currents, stars, and nautical charts, allowed pirates to ply the seas with astonishing precision.

Fact 59 - Pirates and their funny superstitions

Ah, superstitions! Every culture has them, and pirates were not left out, dear reader. Although they were known for their bravery, many of them were also deeply superstitious.

It was common, for example, to think that boarding a ship whistling brought bad luck. The whistling could have unleashed the winds and caused storms, according to their beliefs. Another popular superstition claimed that crossing paths with a black cat before embarking meant a disastrous or unhappy journey.

The women on board were also considered a bad omen, at least for some. They could have distracted the crew or provoked jealousy, thus compromising the cohesion needed to survive at sea. However, some superstitions were more positive, such as that of seeing dolphins playing near the ship, a sign of good luck in perspective.

Superstitions or not, life aboard a pirate ship was unpredictable. But these beliefs offered some solace to these men in the face of the unknown, giving them a semblance of control over their tumultuous destiny.

Fact 60 - The Amazing Friendships Between Pirates and Kings

Imagine, dear reader, a pirate, with his blindfold over his eye and his parrot on his shoulder, chatting gaily with a king in a purple robe in a sumptuous palace. It may seem implausible, but some pirates have indeed forged close ties with monarchs throughout history.

Take Sir Francis Drake as an example. Although he is considered a hero in England, to other nations such as Spain, he was a ruthless pirate. Queen Elizabeth I herself supported him and profited from the treasures he brought back from his expeditions. He was even knighted for his services to the crown.

In other cases, kings used pirates as tools to weaken their enemies. Pirates were then given "letters of marque", which allowed them to attack enemy ships legally. In exchange, they shared their spoils with the crown.

These alliances, as unlikely as they may seem, show that piracy was not always a simple matter of theft and treason. Sometimes it was an integral part of the politics and power games of great nations.

Fact 61 - The Mysterious Treasure of Cocos Island

Have you ever wondered, dear reader, where pirates hide their treasures? Cocos Island, off the coast of Costa Rica, is famous for the stories surrounding pirate treasure supposedly buried there. Many treasure hunters have tried, unsuccessfully, to unearth this fortune, adding to its mystery.

The story goes that the pirate William Thompson hid a colossal booty there in the early 19th century. Captured by the Spaniards, he promised to show the location of the treasure in exchange for his life. However, after bringing some of the crew to the island, he and his men killed them, then escaping with the secret of the treasure.

Since then, many adventurers have tried their luck, including President Franklin Roosevelt. Despite years of searching, no one has been able to locate the treasure. Some believe it could be a legend, while others firmly believe it exists.

Whether it's a fact or a myth, Cocos Island continues to attract explorers from all over the world, all driven by the hope of discovering this mysterious treasure. Who knows, maybe you'll be the next to embark on this thrilling quest?

Fact 62 - Pirates and their singular mascots

Have you ever heard of the curious creatures that pirates used to take aboard their ships? These animals, often exotic, were both companions and status symbols for these daring seafarers. They weren't just there for fun, but also served as valuable distractions on long trips.

Parrots are arguably the most iconic mascots associated with pirates. With their vivid feathers and ability to mimic human speech, these birds were prized additions to any pirate ship. The famous pirate Blackbeard, for example, was often seen with a parrot perched on his shoulder, reinforcing his fearsome image.

But they weren't the only animals on board. Monkeys, in particular, were very popular for their mischievous nature. They were often trained to steal items or to entertain the crew with their antics. Some pirates even had rarer animals, such as leopards or snakes, brought back from distant voyages.

These mascots added a touch of exoticism and mystery to the already adventurous life of pirates. The next time you imagine a pirate, don't forget about his faithful animal companion, who was much more than just an accessory.

Fact 63 - Legendary rivalries between captains

The seas were often the scene of epic battles, but did you know that some of the most memorable were the result of fierce rivalries between pirate captains? These conflicts were sometimes born out of betrayals, ambitions, or simple ego squabbles.

One of the most famous rivalries is that between Captain Blackbeard and Lieutenant Robert Maynard. After several confrontations, their duel culminated in 1718 when Maynard succeeded in ambushing Blackbeard near Ocracoke Island. In an intense battle, Blackbeard was finally defeated, ending his terror on the seas.

Another striking story is that of Bartholomew Roberts and Captain Chaloner Ogle. Roberts, one of the most successful pirates in history, saw his reign come to an end when Ogle hunted him down and shot him in a memorable naval battle in 1722.

But not all rivalries ended in bloodshed. Some captains, such as Charles Vane and Jack Rackham, started out as rivals, but eventually became allies, joining forces to become even more powerful.

These duels and alliances shaped the golden age of piracy, making the pirate story even richer and more captivating.

Fact 64 - Pirates and their frenzied dances

Have you ever wondered how pirates entertain themselves after a long day of looting and boarding? One of their favorite activities was dancing! These dances, often frantic, were an opportunity for them to celebrate their victories, let off steam and forget the dangers of life at sea.

A famous example is the "sword dance". The pirates, armed with their blades, whirled in rhythm, their sabers clashing in a show of skill and bravery. This dance, more than just entertainment, was also a demonstration of their skill in combat.

There was also the "buccaneer's jig," a fast, bouncy dance. Often accompanied by accordion or tambourine, this dance reflected the joy and free spirit of the pirates. It was especially popular at impromptu parties on deserted beaches after a particularly lucrative booty.

So, the next time you picture a pirate, think not only of his epic battles on the high seas, but also of those moments of joy, when, under the stars, he danced without restraint, celebrating freedom and adventure.

Fact 65 - The Secrets of Bottles in the Sea

Maybe you've ever dreamed of finding a bottle in the sea, containing a map leading to a hidden treasure. Well, hackers did use this medium to communicate. But contrary to popular belief, these bottles did not always contain treasure maps.

In reality, hackers often used these bottles as distress messages. If a crew was stranded on a deserted or endangered island, they would throw a bottle into the sea in the hope that it would reach a friendly ship. For example, in 1696, a buccaneer named Thomas Tew threw a bottle containing a message for help after being shipwrecked.

Other times, it was to relay information about enemy movements or warnings to other hackers. It was a rudimentary, but sometimes effective, means of long-distance communication.

So, if one day you come across an old bottle containing a parchment, know that you may be holding in your hands a fragment of pirate history, full of adventure, danger, and secrets.

Fact 66 - Pirates and their underground hideouts

Have you ever imagined that beneath your feet, hidden in the depths of the earth, lies a forgotten pirate treasure? Pirates were masters at the art of concealment, and this includes using underground hideouts to protect their loot.

In reality, the need to hide their treasure stemmed from the constant danger of having it stolen by other pirates or confiscated by the navy. For example, the notorious pirate William Kidd is said to have hidden some of his treasure in an underground cave near the island of Roatán, off the coast of Honduras.

These hideouts were often located on remote islands or isolated coastlines, where pirates dug tunnels or used natural caves to hide their gold, jewelry, and other riches. Death traps were sometimes set to deter anyone from venturing out in search of these treasures.

So, if you ever embark on a treasure hunt, remember that the truth could be buried deep beneath the surface, in the underground hideouts of the pirates of yesteryear.

Fact 67 - Techniques for Evading the Royal Navy

Imagine yourself at the helm of a pirate ship, sails swollen by the wind, with the fearsome Royal Navy hot on your heels. In such a situation, what would you do to escape these determined pursuers? The hackers had their tricks.

One of their favorite techniques was the "jettison". When pursued and in need of speed, pirates threw cannons, cargo, and even fresh water overboard to lighten the ship. The notorious pirate Blackbeard was known to use this method when hunted by warships.

The pirates also knew the waters they were navigating inside out. They used narrow passages, reefs or sandbanks, dangerous for large ships of the Royal Navy, but navigable for their more agile ships. For example, the legendary pirate Jack Rackham eluded his pursuers several times by skilfully navigating through the Caribbean islands.

So, the next time you hear about a pirate miraculously escaping his pursuers, you'll know it wasn't just luck, but also the result of proven seafaring skills and in-depth knowledge of the seas.

Fact 68 - The Lost Treasure of La Buse

You may have heard of pirate treasures that remain untraceable, but do you know the history of the treasure of La Buse? Olivier Levasseur, nicknamed "La Buse", was a feared French pirate who spread terror in the Indian Ocean in the early 18th century.

Rumor has it that just before his execution in 1730, La Buse threw a cryptogram into the crowd, shouting that whoever deciphered it would find his priceless treasure. The document contained strange symbols and drawings that, when decoded, would reveal the exact location of his fortune. Although many have tried, the mystery has never been solved.

Some believe that this treasure is on the island of Mahé in the Seychelles, while others believe that it is hidden on the island of Reunion. Several expeditions were launched to find this legendary treasure, but all ended in failure.

So, if you're feeling like an adventurer and you're passionate about puzzles, maybe the cryptogram of La Buse is waiting for you, concealing the location of one of the greatest treasures ever lost.

Fact 69 - Pirates and Their Extravagant Feasts

Have you ever imagined what pirates might eat when they're not looting ships or searching for treasure? Contrary to popular belief, their diet was not limited to hard bread and rum. When the opportunity arose, pirates knew how to party and feast!

For example, when they landed on tropical islands, they took advantage of exotic fruits such as coconuts, pineapples and mangoes. Add to that the local game and fresh fish, and you have a meal fit for a king. Bartholomew Roberts, a famous pirate, was particularly known for enjoying fine dining, combining different flavors.

It was also not uncommon for pirates to celebrate their victories by throwing real feasts, sometimes cooking whole animals over a bonfire. These moments were an opportunity to share the spoils, sing and dance until dawn.

So, even though the pirate life was hard and perilous, it also offered moments of joy and excess, with feasts that would make many of today's foodies green with envy.

Fact 70 - The Role of Slaves in Pirates

When discussing the history of piracy, the role of slaves is often omitted. Still, they played a significant role in this tumultuous maritime adventure. Contrary to what one might think, their fate among pirate crews was very different from that of slaves in the colonies.

Many pirates, disagreeing with the brutality and injustice of slavery, freed slaves captured during their raids. For example, the famous Blackbeard had several former slaves in his crew, who had become full-fledged members. For these men, piracy offered an unexpected chance for freedom and equality.

Some of these former slaves, once free, even rose through the ranks to become respected captains of pirate ships. One of the most well-known is Black Caesar, who, after escaping slavery, became a fearsome Caribbean pirate.

Thus, even though piracy was far from an ideal world, it sometimes offered a glimmer of hope and redemption to those who had been uprooted from their homeland and enslaved.

Fact 71 - Pirates in the Red Sea

The Red Sea, with its warm waters and strategic sea lanes, has always been a prime location for piracy. Since ancient times, it has attracted sailors of all origins, creating a mix of cultures, but also a fertile ground for illicit activities.

In the 17th century, as the spice and gemstone trade expanded on a large scale, pirates flocked to this lucrative route. A famous pirate from this region is Henry Every, who managed to capture a ship belonging to the great Mughal of India, the "Ganj-i-Sawai", filled with gold, silver, and precious stones. This capture made him famous and, according to some sources, he became the most wanted man of his time.

The Red Sea also offered many natural hiding places, thanks to its reefs and islands, where pirates could hide from patrols. It was a place where alliances were formed and broken, where treasures were found and lost.

But as all good things must come to an end, the increased presence of the British Navy in the 19th century put an end to the golden age of piracy in this region.

Fact 72 - The Pirates' Mysterious Maps

You've probably heard of treasure maps, those worn-out sheets of paper or parchment marked with a cross that indicates where the treasure is hidden. But did you know that many of these cards, if they really existed, contained much deeper mysteries?

Pirates were known for their subterfuge skills. They didn't just draw simple maps. Some say the cards were intentionally misleading, incorporating puzzles or coded symbols to confuse those who were not in the know. For example, the famous pirate Kidd's card, found after his death, was riddled with alchemical symbols that no one has ever been able to decipher.

In addition, these cards were not always made of paper. Stories tell of cards engraved on metal plates, leather, or even tattooed on the skin of one of the crew members! Such a practice ensured that only the pirate's crew knew the exact location of the treasure.

But, of course, the biggest enigma remains whether these treasures have really been discovered, or if, somewhere, a chest full of gold is still waiting to be found thanks to one of these mysterious maps.

Fact 73 - The Secret Life of Black Sam Bellamy

You probably know Black Sam Bellamy as one of the richest pirates in history, but are you aware of the mysteries surrounding his personal life? He was not just a feared pirate, but also a man full of intrigue and secrets.

Bellamy, originally from England, is often referred to as the "Robin Hood of the sea". Before he descended into piracy, he is said to have searched for gold in America in the hope of winning the hand of his beloved, Maria Hallett. Unfortunately, his ambitions were thwarted, pushing him towards a life as a pirate. But, even on the seas, he never forgot Maria and is even said to have returned to her in secret.

Black Sam was also known for his fiery speeches about liberty and equality, criticizing the aristocratic system of the time. Some say he had an account book where he meticulously recorded his share of the booty, proving that he shared wealth fairly with his crew.

Alas, Bellamy's life was short-lived. He died in a storm in 1717, but his legacy and the mysteries surrounding his life continue to fascinate history buffs.

Fact 74 - Techniques for navigating at night

Navigating at night is a delicate art and for pirates, mastering this art was crucial to escape their pursuers or surprise their victims. But how did they precisely manage to navigate in the dark without modern technology?

First, they relied heavily on the stars. The night sky was the pirates' map. The North Star, for example, always pointed north, and the constellations were used as markers to define precise directions. Some pirates even specialized as amateur astronomers to help with navigation.

Then the loch, a speed-measuring instrument, was used. By throwing it into the sea, they could estimate the speed of the ship by counting the time it took to unwind a certain length of rope. This system, although rudimentary, provided an idea of the distance travelled.

Finally, sound also played an essential role. Pirates listened intently to the sounds of the sea, such as whales chirping or waves murmuring against reefs, to detect obstacles or other vessels.

Thanks to these techniques and their intuition, the hackers were formidable navigators, even in total darkness.

Fact 75 - Pirates and Their Unexpected Alliances

When we think of pirates, we imagine lone outlaws sailing the seas in search of treasure. Yet, on many occasions, they have formed surprising alliances to achieve their goals. These collaborations have sometimes changed the course of maritime history.

One of the most famous examples is the alliance between pirates and indigenous peoples. In the Caribbean, pirates such as Blackbeard built relationships with local populations, exchanging goods and information. In return, these communities sometimes provided refuge for pirates or aided them in their attacks on European ships.

Similarly, some hackers have collaborated with governments. Privateers, in particular, were legalized pirates who operated with the support of a nation. Sir Francis Drake, for example, sailed under the patronage of Queen Elizabeth I of England, attacking Spanish ships with her blessing.

These alliances, though unexpected, show the complexity of pirate life. Far from always being isolated outcasts, they knew when and how to forge strategic relationships to maximize their gains and security.

Fact 76 - The Hidden Treasure of the Eastern Seas

Ah, the seas of the Orient! These mysterious waters have fascinated sailors for centuries. But did you know that, according to some legends, they hide one of the most sought-after treasures in pirate history?

One of the region's most feared pirates, Captain Kidd, is said to have hidden a huge treasure in these waters before his arrest in 1699. It is said that, fearing capture by the Royal Navy, he hid some of his booty in a place known only to him and some of his most loyal sailors. Unfortunately for treasure hunters, the exact location remains a mystery to this day.

Many adventurers have tried their luck to find this legendary treasure. Maps were discovered, purporting to show the location of the treasure, but all expeditions ended in failure or minor discoveries. Some even think that the treasure is cursed.

So, if you're feeling adventurous, why not embark on a quest to discover the hidden treasure of the Eastern Seas? But be careful, because these waters are full of wonders as well as dangers.

Fact 77 - Pirates and Their Strange Beliefs

The pirate world is full of legends and superstitions. But have you ever wondered what these sea robbers really believe in?

It is well known that many pirates were superstitious. For example, many considered seeing a black cat aboard a ship to be a bad omen, while others believed that playing music before setting sail brought bad luck. To counter these presumed curses, they often resorted to rituals, such as throwing a coin overboard to appease the spirits of the sea.

But these weren't just mere superstitions. Some pirates believed in the existence of mythical creatures, such as mermaids and the Kraken. The presence of a woman on board was often seen as an opportunity, although other pirates considered it a curse.

Thus, despite their often brutal and pragmatic lives, these privateers were deeply influenced by a world of beliefs and mysteries. These beliefs shaped their daily lives and guided their actions at sea.

Fact 78 - The Secret of Sunken Wrecks

The seabed hides many mysteries, including countless shipwrecks. Have you ever thought about the stories these sunken ships could tell if they could talk?

Many of these shipwrecks are silent witnesses to bloody clashes between pirates and merchant or military ships. One of the most famous is that of the "Whydah Gally", a pirate ship that sank in 1717 near Cape Cod with an immense fortune on board. Rediscovered in 1984, this wreck is a precious testimony to the way of life of the pirates of that time.

However, not all wrecks are the result of battles. Some have fallen victim to the vagaries of nature, trapped by violent storms or betrayed by inaccurate maritime charts. Coral reefs, for example, have been the undoing of many boats that have run aground there, sometimes dooming their crews.

As they dive into the depths, these shipwrecks gradually unveil their secrets, offering researchers and history buffs a fascinating glimpse into the maritime past and pirate adventures.

Fact 79 - Pirates and Their Amazing Remedies

You've probably heard of the hard life of pirates, between battles and long sea voyages. But did you know that these adventurers of the seas had their own remedies to deal with the ills and diseases of their time?

One of the most feared plagues on board was scurvy, caused by a deficiency of vitamin C. To cope with this, some pirates consumed citrus fruits such as lemons or oranges, when they could find them. They had instinctively understood that these fruits prevented this terrible disease.

Pirates also had their own potions to relieve pain, especially during amputations needed after fights. Rum, often associated with pirate life, was commonly used as an anesthetic or to disinfect wounds.

But their remedies didn't stop there. From herbs to animals to strange concoctions, pirates were true alchemists of survival at sea. Their ability to improvise with what they had on hand shows how resilient and resourceful they were.

Fact 80 - The Art of Piracy in the Mediterranean

Did you know that the Mediterranean, with its blue waters and picturesque coastlines, was once a haunt for many pirates? Far from Caribbean piracy, Mediterranean pirates had their own codes and traditions.

The Barbary Indians, for example, were pirates of North African origin who ruled the Mediterranean between the sixteenth and eighteenth centuries. Based in ports such as Algiers, Tunis, and Tripoli, they attacked Christian ships, capturing their crews to demand ransoms or sell them as slaves.

In response to these threats, many European countries built watchtowers along their coasts, to signal the approach of pirates. These towers are still visible today, silent witnesses of a time when the Mediterranean was not always so peaceful.

But these pirates weren't just looters. They were also skilled navigators and traders, maintaining complex networks across the Mediterranean Sea. Through their actions, they have left a lasting mark on the history of this region so rich in cultures and traditions.

Fact 81 - Pirates and Their Funny Hats

Have you ever noticed that when you imagine a pirate, they often wear a distinctive hat? This is no coincidence, as hats played a symbolic and functional role in the lives of pirates.

The tricorne, for example, with its three raised points, was very popular in the seventeenth and eighteenth centuries. In addition to providing protection from the elements, this hat had social significance. It demonstrated the status of the pirate, and the more ornate or extravagant the hat, the more respected and feared the pirate was.

Then there was the headband or scarf. These simple pieces of cloth tied around the head served as protection from the scorching sun and prevented sweat from running into the eyes. But they also had another function: to hide any wounds or scars that these rough men may have suffered in battle.

In the end, pirate hats weren't just fashion accessories. They told a story, the adventures, battles and triumphs of those who bore them with pride on the tumultuous seas.

Fact 82 - Techniques for Taking a Fort

Have you ever wondered how pirates, known primarily for their skills at sea, could storm heavily defended coastal forts? Their methods were cunning and often daring.

The first step was usually a thorough reconnaissance. A small group would sneak up on the fort to study its structure, weak points, and guard routines. They also scouted gun emplacements and searched for hidden approaches for a surprise assault.

Once this information was gathered, the attackers would come up with a plan of attack. In some cases, they used diversionary tactics, such as lighting a fire from a certain distance away to distract the guards. Meanwhile, a group of pirates silently infiltrated the fort.

Another common technique was the massive, sudden attack. The pirates relied on the element of surprise and their numbers to quickly overwhelm the fort's defenses.

Regardless of the method used, the objective was always the same: to quickly capture the fort, secure the area, and seize any treasures or resources inside.

Fact 83 - The Pirate Oliver's Lost Treasure

You've probably heard of many famous pirates and their hidden treasures, but do you know the story of the pirate Olivier and his elusive treasure? It's an enigma that has fascinated treasure hunters for centuries.

Olivier was a feared pirate in the early 18th century. Unlike other pirates of his time, he had a predilection for art objects and precious stones. He plundered not only ships, but also mansions and palaces along the coasts.

It is said that after years of looting, Olivier buried his treasure on a remote island in the Caribbean. An intriguing peculiarity of this legend is the so-called "Owl Map", a cryptic map that Olivier is said to have created to mark the location of his treasure.

Although many adventurers have attempted to track down Oliver's treasure using this map, none have been successful so far. The treasure of the pirate Olivier remains one of the great unsolved mysteries of the golden age of piracy. Who knows, maybe you'll be the next one to try your luck?

Fact 84 - Pirates and Their Codes of Honor

When we think of pirates, we often imagine ruthless and unprincipled outlaws. However, did you know that many of them lived by strict codes of honor? Yes, even in the lawless world of piracy, honor had its place.

For example, the famous pirate Blackbeard had a set of rules that each member of his crew had to follow. These rules stipulated things such as not playing dice or cards, how to divide the spoils, and how to conduct themselves in battles. Anyone who broke these rules could be abandoned on a desert island or, in extreme cases, executed.

Another example is the code of the pirate Bartholomew Roberts, which insisted on the importance of sobriety on board. According to him, a drunken pirate was a threat to the entire crew. Roberts even went so far as to ban alcohol consumption altogether the night before an attack.

These codes of honor were essential for maintaining order and discipline among pirate crews. They show that, even in a world of violence and betrayal, certain principles remained sacred.

Fact 85 - The Riddles of the Lost Islands

Tales of hidden treasures and lost islands have always captured the imagination. And in the pirate world, these stories were more than legends: they were realities that attracted adventurers and treasure hunters. You, too, have probably wondered if these mysterious islands really exist.

Take the example of the island of Tromelin, discovered in the 18th century after the sinking of a French ship. Located in the Indian Ocean, this island remained isolated for decades, with only a few survivors of the shipwreck who had found refuge there. Their existence was only a rumor until a French expedition discovered them years later.

There's also the fascinating history of Oak Island, Canada. Since the 19th century, treasure hunters have been convinced that pirate treasure is buried there, after discovering a series of elaborate clues and traps. Despite the efforts, the treasure remains elusive.

These islands, with their unsolved mysteries, are a testament to the enduring appeal of pirate stories. Even if some remain enigmas, the adventure of discovery continues to ignite imaginations.

Fact 86 - The Mystery of the Pirates of the Caribbean

Ah, the Caribbean! When we think of these paradise islands, you probably imagine fine sandy beaches and turquoise waters. But, in the past, they were the favorite playground of the most fearsome pirates. Their history in this region is tinged with mystery and adventure.

One of the most famous pirates of the Caribbean was the dreaded Blackbeard. His ship, the "Queen Anne's Revenge", terrorized the seas. Yet, despite his notoriety, many aspects of his life remain mysterious. For example, its abrupt end near North Carolina in 1718 is still debated among historians.

The Caribbean Sea holds other enigmas, such as that of the "Flying Dutchman", the ghost ship doomed to wander forever. Although considered a legend, many sailors have sworn to have crossed paths with it on stormy nights.

Behind the apparent calm of the Caribbean waters, there are incredible stories of piracy. Each island, each bay could tell you a different adventure, if only the waves could talk. These mysteries continue to fascinate and inspire entire generations.

Fact 87 - Pirates and Their Funny Names

Maybe you've noticed, but pirates often had rather original and sometimes even comical nicknames. These pseudonyms, in addition to adding a touch of mystery, served to mask their true identity or to enhance their reputation among sailors.

Let's take the example of "Blackbeard". His real name was Edward Teach, but his nickname, far more intimidating, alluded to his large, thick black beard that gave him a fearsome look. This name was so iconic that it is now much more famous than its real name.

There was also "Calico Jack," whose original name was John Rackham. His nickname came from his preference for clothing made of calico, a type of fabric. Or "Black Dog", a fictional character, whose mysterious name is enough to provoke fear.

These nicknames, while sometimes amusing, were essential in the world of piracy. They not only concealed an identity but also created legends that survived far beyond the life of the pirate himself.

Fact 88 - Techniques for hoisting the sails

Have you ever wondered how pirates manage to sail with these huge sails on their ships? Hoisting a sail was not a simple matter; This required competence, strength and coordination.

First, the sail had to be properly folded and stored for quick deployment. When the captain gave the order, the crew rushed to the deck, stationing themselves at strategic points. They used specific ropes, called "sheets" and "halyards", to control the vertical and horizontal movement of the sails.

The crew worked in tandem, hoisting the sail with the help of these ropes. For example, hoisting the mainsail of a ship like Blackbeard's "Queen Anne's Revenge" required impeccable coordination of several men. Sea shanties, which you may have heard, were often used to synchronize these efforts.

The process of hoisting the sails was essential for fast and efficient navigation. By mastering this technique, pirates could not only pursue their prey but also evade their pursuers, thus securing a feared place on the seas.

Fact 89 - Pirates and their adventures in Africa

When you think of pirates, you probably picture epic battles in the Caribbean. But did you know that Africa was also a popular destination for these buccaneers? The African coasts were full of riches and challenges for these adventurers of the seas.

The west coast of Africa was a strategic location for trade, especially because of the Gold Route, which offered pirates great opportunities for booty. Bartholomew Roberts, for example, captured the Portuguese ship "Sagrado Coração" near Cape Lopez, taking with it thousands of pounds in gold.

In addition, African waters were also the playground of the Barbary pirates. Based in North Africa, these Muslim privateers terrorized European ships, capturing not only goods but also prisoners to ransom or sell them as slaves.

These incursions into Africa demonstrate that piracy was not limited to a single region. In search of riches and adventure, pirates roamed the world, leaving their mark wherever they went.

Fact 90 - Henry Avery's Hidden Treasure

Henry Avery, sometimes referred to as "The Pirate King", is one of the most famous names in piracy. Its notoriety is based not only on its looting, but also on the enigma surrounding its missing treasure. Let me tell you his story.

In 1695, Avery and his crew made one of the most daring robberies in the history of piracy. They attacked and took control of the "Ganj-i-Sawai", a ship belonging to the great Mughal of India, with an estimated fortune of £600,000 on board, a colossal sum for the time.

But after this spectacular move, Avery disappeared from the radar. Rumours circulated that he had retired to the Caribbean or that he had settled under a false identity in England. No one knows exactly where he hid his loot, and many treasure hunters have tried in vain to locate him.

Today, Henry Avery's treasure remains one of piracy's greatest mysteries. Who knows? Maybe you'll be the one to finally discover its hidden riches!

Fact 91 - Pirates and Their Amazing Customs

When you think of pirates, you probably picture adventures at sea, treasures, and battles. But did you know that they also have their own amazing traditions and customs? Let's dive into this fascinating world.

One of the most surprising customs was the "pirate law". Before embarking on an adventure, the crew would often establish a code of conduct that everyone had to abide by. For example, any crew member who stole another member was abandoned on a deserted island. It was a way to ensure loyalty and mutual trust on board.

Another amazing tradition was the "fair share". The booty was divided equally among all the pirates in the crew. The captain and officers usually received a larger share, but each pirate was entitled to his piece of the pie. This fairness enhanced the sense of camaraderie.

Finally, pirates had a unique way of sealing pacts. Instead of signing documents, they cut off the palms of their hands and mixed their blood, symbolizing their brotherhood. These customs, while barbaric in our eyes, strengthened the bonds between the pirates and made them stronger as a group.

Fact 92 - The Secrets of Pirate Honeymoons

When you think of a honeymoon, you probably picture white sand beaches and romantic sunsets. But have you ever thought about how pirates celebrate their unions? Let's discover together these honeymoons like no other.

Pirates, despite their lives of adventure and danger, were also looking for love. When they found their soulmate, they did not hesitate to marry at sea, often with improvised ceremonies, led by the ship's captain. After the exchange of vows, the party was in full swing with singing, dancing and, of course, plenty of rum.

Their honeymoon, on the other hand, wasn't always what we'd call romantic. Sometimes, the newlywed couple would share a series of adventures, such as searching for treasure or conquering an island. These shared moments strengthened their bond and forged unforgettable memories.

However, a few lucky pirates managed to find moments of tranquility, treating themselves to a few days on a secluded island, out of sight, to celebrate their union. These parentheses were rare, but they showed that even in the tumultuous life of a pirate, love had its place.

Fact 93 - Pirates and their unique coats of arms

You've probably seen black flags fluttering in the wind, adorned with skulls and crossed shins. But did you know that each pirate often had their own coat of arms, as unique as their fingerprint? Let's dive into this universe of symbols together.

The famous Jolly Roger with his skull and bones became emblematic of piracy, but he was not the only emblem used. Some pirates, eager to stand out, created distinctive coats of arms. For example, Calico Jack had a flag depicting a skull surmounted by two crossed swords.

These coats of arms were not just decorations. They had a strategic function. By raising their distinctive flag, pirates would announce their identities to their potential victims, often sparking fear and surrender without a fight. It was a form of psychology of war before its time.

So, as you sailed through the seas of the past, you could have seen an astonishing variety of flags flying on pirate ships. Each told a story, presented a threat, and revealed a bit of its owner's personality.

Fact 94 - Techniques for Building a Ship

Building a ship in the pirate era was an art, combining expertise and ingenuity. Do you know how these floating masterpieces were assembled?

It all started with the choice of wood. Oak, strong and durable, was preferred for the hull. Forests were abundantly exploited to provide these valuable materials. A ship, like Blackbeard's famous "Queen Anne's Revenge," could require hundreds of trees.

Once the wood was selected, the next step was the framing, the backbone of the ship. The ribs were then attached to this frame, giving the ship its distinct shape. Shipwrights, armed with their tools and knowledge, played a crucial role here.

Finally, the hull was covered with planks, carefully fitted and caulked to ensure watertightness. But the ship was not yet ready to set sail. Masts, sails, ropes and cannons completed the ensemble, transforming this pile of wood into a formidable machine of war or commerce.

The next time you hear about a pirate ship, imagine the colossal amount of work behind its construction. Every board, every knot, every detail has its own story.

Fact 95 - Pirates and their incredible challenges

Pirates, contrary to what one might think, did not spend all their time plundering ships. They also took on incredible challenges, proving their courage and boldness. Do you know what those extraordinary challenges were?

The first notable challenge was navigating uncharted waters. The ocean was a vast and mysterious territory, and maps were not always accurate. Pirates like William Dampier explored pristine territories, braving storms and unknown reefs to forge new routes.

Then there was the challenge of combat. It was not only a question of strength, but also of strategy. Bartholomew Roberts, for example, took more than 400 ships during his career, displaying remarkable tactical skill.

But the challenges didn't stop there. Some pirates have even attempted to create their own colonies or "pirate republics", such as that of Libertalia in Madagascar, although its historical reality is debated.

Whenever you think of pirates, remember the colossal challenges they overcame. Their lives were not only made up of treasures and battles, but also daring adventures and never-before-seen quests.

Fact 96 - The Lost Treasure of the Persian Gulf

You've probably heard of buried treasures in the Caribbean or the New World, but did you know that there are also stories of lost treasures in the Persian Gulf? Yes, this region also has its mysteries and legends.

In the 17th century, a notorious pirate named Rahmah ibn Jabir al-Jalahimah was rampant in the Persian Gulf. Known for his cruelty and ingenuity, Rahmah amassed an immense fortune through his daring raids on merchant ships.

Rumor has it that in the twilight of her life, fearing to lose her treasure to her enemies or traitors, Rahmah hid some of her loot on a remote island in the Gulf. Although many adventurers have attempted to locate this fortune, it remains untraceable to this day.

Perhaps, one day, you will be the lucky discoverer of this legendary treasure? But remember, the pirate world is full of danger and betrayal. Searching for treasure requires courage, perseverance, and a dash of luck.

Fact 97 - Pirates and their tricks to survive

Have you ever imagined the harsh and unpredictable life of a pirate? These sea brigands didn't just have to fear enemy ships or bounty hunters. Survival on a day-to-day basis was a challenge in itself, and they had a few tricks at their disposal.

First, to avoid scurvy, a common disease among sailors caused by vitamin C deficiency, pirates consumed citrus fruits when they could. For example, the famous Blackbeard was often seen chewing a lemon to keep his strength. Citrus fruits were a prized possession on board, not only for their taste, but also for their healing properties.

The pirates also had their own methods of obtaining fresh water. Some used tarps or sails to collect rainwater, while others had the trick of drinking the turtles' blood, which was slightly salty but drinkable.

Finally, to heal wounds, many used rum or hard liquor as a disinfectant. It burned, but it was often the only remedy available. So, despite a lifetime of constant danger, these pirates knew how to adapt and make the most of what they had on hand.

Fact 98 - The Riddles of the Missing Ships

Did you know that the history of piracy is littered with unexplained mysteries and ships that have disappeared without a trace? These disappearances have become legends, arousing curiosity and fascination.

One of the most famous is the "Phantom of the Sea". Leaving England in 1723 with a precious cargo, it never arrived at its destination. Despite an intense search, no wreckage or trace of the crew was found. Some whisper that the captain had made a pact with supernatural forces to protect his treasure.

Then there is the disappearance of the "Sirena Dorada" in 1798, a Spanish ship carrying an immense fortune. Witnesses claimed to have seen it caught in a storm, but when rescuers arrived at the scene, the sea was calm and there was no sign of the ship.

There is also mention of the "Black Shadow", which disappeared in the waters of the Caribbean in 1632. There are many legends surrounding this ship, including that it was cursed by a voodoo sorcerer for stealing a sacred artifact.

These puzzles, among many others, are a reminder that the world of pirates is rich in mysteries and adventures, where reality and legend are closely intertwined.

Fact 99 - Pirates and Their Incredible Legends

Have you ever heard of the fascinating legends that have plagued the seas, fueled by pirates, sailors and travellers? These stories, often mixed with reality and myth, still captivate our imagination today.

Take, for example, the legend of the Kraken, a gigantic sea creature described as having long tentacles capable of engulfing entire ships. Pirates from the time of the "Golden Sea" claimed to have spotted it, creating palpable fear among the crews.

Then there's Death Island, a place that was said to be cursed. Rumor has it that any pirate who landed on the island never left. Blackbeard himself is said to have warned his crew never to venture there, fearing his evil power.

Finally, the legend of the Flying Dutchman, the ghost ship doomed to wander eternally on the oceans. Sailors swore they had seen him, suddenly appearing in the mist before disappearing just as quickly.

Every legend has some truth to it, and it's this ambiguity that makes the pirate world so mesmerizing and eternal.

Fact 100 - The Art of Piracy Through the Ages

Piracy, contrary to what you might think, is not a phenomenon limited to one time or region. It has evolved through the ages, adapting its techniques and codes to its environment.

In the time of the ancient Greeks and Romans, pirates were already plying the Mediterranean. One of the most famous, Dionysius the Phocaean, used oars and sails to quickly surprise his prey. Techniques were based on cunning and speed.

In the Middle Ages, Viking pirates dominated the North Seas, using their fast and light longships to conduct lightning raids on the coasts of Europe. Their reputation as fearsome warriors preceded them, sowing terror among coastal populations.

The Golden Age of Piracy, in the 17th and 18th centuries, saw the emergence of legendary figures like Blackbeard and Calico Jack, using heavily armed ships to challenge the great maritime powers.

Through each era, the art of piracy has evolved, but one constant remains: the desire for adventure, wealth and freedom that drives these men and women to defy laws and oceans.

Conclusion

And so, sailor of knowledge, the journey through the tumultuous oceans of piracy is coming to an end. Together, we sailed through stories, legends and truths, discovering the darkest and most heroic facets of these outlaws of the seas. If you've felt the thrill of adventure, the excitement of treasure hunting, or admiration for these pirates with exceptional destiny, then this trip has reached its goal.

But remember, every story, every incredible fact you've discovered is just the tip of the iceberg. History is vast, as are the oceans, and there are still so many treasures to discover. Pirates, with their insatiable thirst for freedom and adventure, remind us that sometimes you have to dare to think outside the box, to take risks, to truly live.

So, wherever you are, keep that pirate spirit inside you. Always seek adventure, be curious and bold. And who knows, maybe one day you, too, will discover a hidden treasure, whether it's made of gold or unforgettable memories. May the winds be favorable to you, and may your horizon always be filled with new adventures to live!

Marc Dresgui

Quiz

1) Why was it so crucial for pirates to hoist the sails correctly?

    a) To appear intimidating.
    b) To avoid storms.
    c) To optimize the speed and manoeuvrability of the vessel.
    d) To report their position to other vessels.

2) Which famous pirate has a treasure that is still being sought after in the Persian Gulf?

    a) Jack Sparrow.
    b) Henry Avery.
    c) Blackbeard.
    d) Calico Jack.

3) What were pirate flags most often a symbol of?

    a) Peace and negotiation.
    b) Wealth and prosperity.
    c) Of threats and deaths.
    d) From their country of origin.

4) Where have pirates had notable adventures besides the Caribbean?

    a) In the Arctic.

b) In the Mediterranean.
c) In Africa.
d) In the Black Sea.

5) How did the pirates ensure good cohesion on board?

a) By throwing parties every night.
b) By following a code of honor.
c) By avoiding any form of discipline.
d) By recruiting only family members.

6) What is a common survival tactic used by hackers?

a) Deep meditation.
b) Consumption of poisonous plants.
c) Use of treasure maps.
d) Knowledge of ocean currents and winds.

7) What maritime enigma has never been solved?

a) The mystery of flying boats.
b) The location of Oliver's treasure.
c) The disappearance of ships on the high seas.
d) The construction of the first ships.

8) How did pirates often name their ships?

a) According to ancient legends.

b) With funny or ironic names.

c) Based on their favorite food.

d) Depending on their country of origin.

9) What element was NOT a typical custom among pirates?

a) Marry the crew members.

b) Divide the loot fairly.

c) Wear symbolic tattoos.

d) Play the game of "dart launcher".

10) What kind of loot did the Persian Gulf pirates primarily seek?

a) Beads.

b) Gold.

c) Rare fish.

d) Silk garments.

11) How did pirates secure their supply of fresh water?

a) By digging wells on each island.

b) By capturing mermaids.

c) By filtering seawater.

d) By storing rain and finding sources of fresh water on the islands.

12) How did pirates treat the merchant ships they attacked?

    a) They were always sinking them.
    b) They were taking them hostage.
    c) They stole them, but often left the crews alive.
    d) They turned them into pirate ships.

13) Which famous pirate is known to have hidden a treasure that remains untraceable?

    a) Captain Kidd.
    b) Edward Teach.
    c) Jack Rackham.
    d) Anne Bonny.

14) How were female pirates viewed among their male counterparts?

    a) Like mascots.
    b) With the same respect as men.
    c) Like jinx.
    d) They were completely forbidden on board.

15) Which pirate is associated with the riddle of the Lost Islands?

    a) Blackbeard.
    b) Charles Vane.

c) Olivier Levasseur.
   d) Bartholomew Roberts.

16) Why did pirates avoid sailing in the Arctic?
   a) Too many sirens.
   b) Not enough loot.
   c) Icy waters and treacherous conditions.
   d) They didn't like the cold.

17) How did pirates party after a victory?
   a) By lighting a large fire.
   b) Dancing under the moon.
   c) By playing hide and seek.
   d) By meditating.

18) What food was crucial for pirates' sea voyages?
   a) Dried fish.
   b) Apples.
   c) Hard biscuits or "galettes de mer".
   d) Berries.

19) How did pirates orient themselves at sea before the invention of the compass?
   a) They used magic compasses.
   b) They followed the stars and the position of the sun.

c) They were asking the dolphins for directions.
   d) They used cards drawn by witches.

20) What tactics did hackers use to avoid unnecessary conflict?

   a) Dress up as mermaids.
   b) Sing soothing songs.
   c) Use flags of various colors to communicate their intentions.
   d) Send messenger pigeons.

Answers

1) Why was it so crucial for pirates to hoist the sails correctly?

Correct answer: c)To optimize the speed and manoeuvrability of the vessel.

2) Which famous pirate has a treasure that is still being sought after in the Persian Gulf?

Correct answer: (b) Henry Avery.

3) What were pirate flags most often a symbol of?

Correct answer: c) Of threats and death.

4) Where have pirates had notable adventures besides the Caribbean?

Correct answer: (c) In Africa.

5) How did the pirates ensure good cohesion on board?

Correct answer: b) By following a code of honor.

6) What is a common survival tactic used by hackers?

Correct answer: (d) Knowledge of ocean currents and winds.

7) What maritime enigma has never been solved?

Correct answer: (c) The disappearance of ships on the high seas.

8) How did pirates often name their ships?

Correct answer: b) With funny or ironic names.

9) What element was NOT a typical custom among pirates?

Correct answer: d) Play the game of "dart launcher".

10) What kind of loot did the Persian Gulf pirates primarily seek?

Correct answer: a) Pearls.

11) How did pirates secure their supply of fresh water?

Correct answer: d) By storing rain and finding fresh water sources on the islands.

12) How did pirates treat the merchant ships they attacked?

Correct answer: c) They stole them, but often left the crews alive.

13) Which famous pirate is known to have hidden a treasure that remains untraceable?

Correct answer: a) Captain Kidd.

14) How were female pirates viewed among their male counterparts?

Correct answer: b) With the same respect as men.

15) Which pirate is associated with the riddle of the Lost Islands?

Correct answer: (c) Olivier Levasseur.

16) Why did pirates avoid sailing in the Arctic?

Correct answer: (c) Icy waters and treacherous conditions.

17) How did pirates party after a victory?

Correct answer: b) Dancing under the moon.

18) What food was crucial for pirates' sea voyages?

Correct answer: c) Hard biscuits or "galettes de mer".

19) How did pirates orient themselves at sea before the invention of the compass?

Correct answer: b) They followed the stars and the position of the sun.

20) What tactics did hackers use to avoid unnecessary conflict?

Correct answer: c) Use flags of various colours to communicate their intentions.

Printed in Great Britain
by Amazon